I0626871

Stage Ready Tales for Creative Youth

Inspiring Youth with Couplets - Vol 6

Created by

metaScreenPlays LLC

Preface

Welcome parents, teachers, daycare aides, and lovers of the Arts - to Volume 6 of Stage Ready Tales for Creative Youth!

Here is where the curtain rises on a brand-new season of imagination, creativity, and show-stopping performances!

As we take our next step on this thrilling journey, we're building on the foundations laid in our previous volumes. Get ready for:

More daring themes and topics that ignite young passions

Even more complex and captivating couplets tailored for our growing stars

Expanded resources for parents, educators, and young performers to fuel their creative fires.

Our mission remains unchanged: to empower the next generation of creative thinkers, confident performers, and passionate storytellers. Join us as we shine the spotlight on the incredible talents of our young artists!

Let the shows begin!

Engaging with Children's Couplets

This description aims to guide you in using this delightful children's book of couplets as a multifaceted tool for entertainment, skill development, and enjoyment. Many of our stories are based on Aesop's Fables and written as live-stage scripts. Whether you're reading aloud at home, facilitating a classroom activity, nurturing public speaking skills, or performing a production, these couplets can foster creativity and confidence in young minds and inspire creativity in sharing entertaining messages.

Directions for Use

1. Reading Aloud

Create a Routine: Set aside a specific time each day for reading. This fosters anticipation and excitement.

Engage with Expression: Encourage animated reading. Use different voices for characters and emphasize rhythm and rhyme to make the experience lively.

2. Public Speaking Skills

Practice Recitations: Choose a few couplets for children to memorize and recite. This builds confidence and helps with articulation.

Encourage Performance: Organize a mini talent show where children can perform their chosen couplets, allowing them to express themselves in front of an audience.

3. Acting and Directing

Role Play: Assign roles for different couplets and let children act them out. This promotes teamwork and creativity. Words or phrases can be replaced, as long as it makes sense with the production goals.

Directing Exercises: Teach children basic directing skills by having them guide their peers on how to perform their couplets, focusing on tone, body language, and pacing. Everyone may not want to act.

Stage Management: Show students how to manage the talent, schedules and remove obstacles for a successful production.

4. Enhancing Reading Skills

Phonemic Awareness: Use the rhymes to highlight sounds and syllables. This can help improve phonetic skills and vocabulary.

Discussion Prompts: After reading, ask questions about the couplets to enhance comprehension and critical thinking.

5. Fostering Enjoyment

Creative Extensions: Encourage children to create their own couplets, allowing them to explore language and storytelling.

Illustration Activities: Have children illustrate their favorite couplets, combining art and literature for a richer experience.

Conclusion

By weaving together fun and learning through this collection of couplets and stories, you can create memorable experiences that enhance literacy, speaking skills, and a love for language. Enjoy the journey of discovery and creativity with all of our readers!

Happy reading and acting!

metaScreenPlays - Learn, Create, Inspire

metaScreenPlays@gmail.com

Dedicated to our second son, who has prepared himself as a Financial professional and musician (tenor sax and keyboards). I'm so proud of you and love you very much. Keep living in your positive light and sharing your knowledge and creativity with the youth. You continue to impress us and our community.

Thanks to our talented artists:

- skooma04 (on all platforms)
- Natasha - natashanancy2333@gmail.com

R. Connor

Table of Contents

THE EAGLE AND HIS CAPTOR

Characters needed:

- Narrator
- Fox

Narrator:

A man once caught an Eagle and, after clipping his wings, turned him loose among the chickens in his hen-house, where he moped in a corner, looking very dejected and helpless.

After a while, his Captor was glad enough to sell him to a neighbor, who took him home and let his wings grow again.

As soon as he had recovered the use of his powerful wings, the Eagle flew out and caught a fat rabbit, which he brought home and presented to his new owner.

A fox observed this and said to the Eagle,

Fox:

Why waste your energy and gifts on him!

Your reason is obvious, but the logic is dim.

You should go and give gifts to the man who first caught you;

He is the one you should befriend and give fresh rabbits to.

You better keep an eye on him. What he did to you is a crime.

Else, he may catch you again and clip your wings a second time.

Moral: Rewarding the right person for their deeds is like watering the correct plant; it encourages growth, fosters fairness, and brings forth a harvest of trust and integrity.

tHe eNd

True strength lies in freedom and the ability to make our own choices. The eagle in the story is able to demonstrate its true strength and power only when it is free from captivity and able to exercise its natural abilities. This story teaches us the importance of valuing our individuality and independence and thinking logically about how we spend our time.

Notes Page

Couplet Title:

_____

What I Learned:

_____

_____

_____

My Favorite Line:

_____

_____

_____

How I Can Apply This:

_____

_____

_____

Draw a Picture:

Additional Thoughts:

_____

_____

_____

THE WORKERS AND THE SEED PHRASE

Characters needed:

- Narrator
- First man
- Companion

Narrator:

Two men were cleaning out an old storage room when one of them picked up a silver case. He opened the case and pulled out an old yellow piece of paper. On the delicate piece of paper were twenty-four words and the name of an old digital wallet application.

First man:

How lucky I am! I think my ship has finally come in! I think

I have found someone's seed phrase! And judging by the looks of this silver case and the paper's age, it must be full of cryptocurrency.

Companion:

Hold on, friend. We are here working together. I am the one who told you about this job! Do not say, 'I think my ship has finally come in' and 'I have found someone's seed phrase.' That is not the whole story.

First man:

Oh really? I gave you a ride here. So, what should I say?
What's the whole story?

Companion

You should say: 'I think OUR ship has finally come in'
and 'WE have found someone's seed phrase' and how
lucky 'WE are.' I know finders are keepers, but I'm here
also, working right beside you. We should share the good
and the bad. I would share whatever I found with you.

First man:

No, no, I don't believe that! You are trying to trick me out
of my dream and the loot I found. I found it, and I am going
to keep it. Like you said, finders are keepers.

Narrator:

So the man took out his cell phone and logged into the wallet application and started transferring all the digital wallet's contents into his own wallet.

First man:

I'm rich, I'm rich! Look at this crypto going into my wallet!

Companion:

You don't deserve all that alone, you should share with me, since I told you about this job and I was helping you! Pause the transaction and let me get some.

First man:

No, No. You must be crazy! You can't pause a transaction. I'm not letting you get anything. But I will hire you. Complete cleaning out this room. I quit! LOL

Narrator:

Just then they heard a loud noise from the man's cell phone, similar to an Amber alert. The cell phone started beeping and began to violently vibrate. A message ran across the screen to stand by for arrest, and the FBI is on the way to this GPS coordinate. A second later, they heard a helicopter and a loudspeaker telling them to vacate the storage room by walking out backward with hands up, and bringing the silver case and cell phone out.

The man who had found the seed phrases fell into a panic.

First man:

How did they get here that fast?! Our lives are ruined if they find this silver case and cell phone on us. What are we going to do?

Companion:

Whoa. No, no, friend. You would not say 'our' and 'us' before, so keep sticking to and saying your 'I.' Say, 'My life is ruined if they find this silver case and my cell phone on me.' …Yessir, I am coming out with my hands up. You can check the silver case and cell phone for fingerprints. I am innocent, don't shoot!

Moral: *We cannot expect anyone to share our misfortunes unless we are willing to share our good fortune also.*

tHe eNd

What is a Seed Phrase?

A seed phrase is a special list of words that helps keep your online accounts and digital money safe. It's like a secret code that only you know.

Why is it Important?

Imagine you forget the password to your favorite online game or your digital wallet. If you have a seed phrase, you can use it to get back into your account. It's like having a spare key to your online stuff.

How Does it Work?

When you create a new account or digital wallet, you'll usually be given a seed phrase. It's a list of 12 or 24 words that you need to keep safe. If you ever need to recover your account, you'll use this seed phrase to prove it's really you.

What Should I Do with My Seed Phrase?

Here are some important tips:

1. Keep it secret: Don't tell anyone your seed phrase, not even your best friend!

2. Store it safely: Write it down and keep it in a safe place, like a locked box or a secret hiding spot.

3. Make a copy: Make a copy of your seed phrase and store it in a different safe place, just in case.

Remember, your seed phrase is like a superpower that keeps your online stuff safe. Be careful with it, and it will help keep your digital life secure!

Notes Page

Couplet Title:

_____

What I Learned:

_____

_____

_____

My Favorite Line:

_____

_____

_____

How I Can Apply This:

_____

_____

_____

Draw a Picture:

Additional Thoughts:

_____

_____

_____

THE FISHERMAN AND THE LITTLE FISH

Characters needed:

- Narrator

- Fish

- Fisherman

Narrator:

A hungry Fisherman, who lived on the fish he caught, had bad luck one day and caught nothing but a very small fry. The Fisherman was about to put it in his basket when the little fish said:

Fish:

Please spare me, Mr. Fisherman! You don't want to waste your time with me. Throw me back in the water. I am so tiny and small it is not worth your time to carry me home. When I am older and bigger, I shall make you a much better meal.

Narrator:

But the Fisherman quickly put the fish into his basket anyway.

Fisherman:

You must think I'm crazy. Throw you back in the water? LOL. Not worth my time to carry you home? LOL. However small you may be, you are better than nothing at all.

Moral: *A small gain is worth more than a large promise.*

tHe eNd

Real-Life Examples:

1. Allowance: Imagine your parents promise to give you a huge allowance next month, but they're not sure if they can afford it. Versus, your neighbor offers to pay you $10 right now to walk their dog. Which one would you choose?

2. School Project: Your friend promises to help you with a big school project, but they're really busy and might not follow through. Versus, your classmate offers to help you with a smaller task, like studying for a quiz, and they're available to help you right away.

3. Savings: You might promise yourself that you'll save $100 next month, but you're not sure if you'll be able to. Versus, you could start saving $5 each week, which is a smaller amount, but it's something you can definitely do.

Historical/Famous Examples:

1. The Story of the Goose That Laid the Golden Eggs: A farmer owned a goose that laid golden eggs. He was impatient and wanted all the eggs at once, so he killed the goose. But, if he had waited and taken one egg at a time, he would have had a steady supply of golden eggs.

2. The Tortoise and the Hare: The tortoise might have promised himself that he would win the race by a huge margin, but instead, he focused on taking small, steady steps and eventually won the race.

Discussion Questions:

1. Can you think of a time when you chose a small gain over a large promise? How did it turn out?

2. Why do you think it's often better to choose a small gain over a large promise?

3. How can you apply this moral to your everyday life?

Notes Page

Couplet Title:

_____

What I Learned:

_____

_____

_____

My Favorite Line:

_____

_____

_____

How I Can Apply This:

_____

_____

_____

Draw a Picture:

Additional Thoughts:

_____

_____

_____

THE ASS AND THE LAPDOG

Characters needed:

- Narrator

- Ass

- Lapdog

- Owner

Narrator:

Once upon a time, an ass was walking by a house and saw a lapdog living a comfortable life inside. Food in one bowl, fresh clean water in the other, and a customized doggy bed with a pillow.

Ass:

Whoa, that lapdog has it good! A bed and food just lying there? I wish I could live like that. I think I can change my ways. In fact, I know I can change my ways. I can live like that!

Narrator:

The ass decided that he wanted to be a lapdog too, and so he barged into the house. He had mud on his hoofs, smelled bad, and ten flies buzzed around him.

Owner:

What is that smell? What is this on my clean rug? Get out of my house, you donkey!

Ass:

Wait, I just want to be a lapdog like that one over there. Hi friend!

Lapdog:

I do not know you! Who is this brute? He's much too big to be a lapdog.

Owner: (to Ass)

You can't just come in here and demand to be my lapdog! You and your flies have to go!

Ass:

But I want to be comfortable like that lapdog! I can be loyal!

Narrator:

The owner knew the ass was too big, stinky, and heavy to be a lapdog, and so he kicked him out of the house.

Ass: (to himself)

I guess I'm just an ass and will never be as comfortable as that lapdog.

Narrator:

The moral of the story: *People should not try to pretend to be something they are not.*

tHe eNd

Real-Life Examples:

1. Faking a Hobby: Imagine you're trying out for a school club, and you claim to be an expert at playing the guitar, but you've never actually played before. Versus, being honest and saying you're interested in learning.

2. Impressing Friends: You might try to pretend to be a great athlete to impress your friends, but you're actually not very good at sports. Versus, being honest about your abilities and finding other ways to connect with your friends.

3. Social Media: You might post fake or exaggerated updates on social media to make it seem like you're having a more exciting life than you really are. Versus, being authentic and sharing your real experiences.

Historical/Famous Examples:

1. The Story of the Ugly Duckling: A duckling tried to fit in with the other ducks by pretending to be something he was not. But he eventually found acceptance and happiness by being himself.

2. The Emperor's New Clothes: A king pretended to wear magnificent clothes that didn't actually exist. He was afraid to admit the truth, but eventually, a child pointed out the reality.

Discussion Questions:

1. Can you think of a time when you tried to pretend to be something you're not? How did it make you feel?

2. Why do you think it's important to be authentic and true to yourself?

3. How can you apply this moral to your everyday life, especially in situations where you might feel pressure to pretend to be something you're not?

Additional Tips:

1. Embrace Your Uniqueness: Celebrate what makes you different and special.

2. Be Honest: It's okay to say, "I don't know," or "I'm not good at that."

3. Find Your True Friends: Surround yourself with people who accept and appreciate you for who you are.

Notes Page

Couplet Title:

_____

What I Learned:

_____

_____

_____

My Favorite Line:

_____

_____

_____

How I Can Apply This:

_____

_____

_____

Draw a Picture:

Additional Thoughts:

_____

_____

_____

THE HARES AND THE FOXES

Characters needed:

- Narrator

- Hare 1

- Hare 2

- Fox 1

- Fox 2

Narrator:

In a forest, there were many hares and foxes who lived together in relative peace. One day, one hare said to another.

Hare 1: (to Hare 2)

I'm getting tired of always being afraid of the foxes.

Hare 2: (to Hare 1)

What do you mean? They haven't bothered us.

Narrator:

The hares decided to confront the foxes about their anxieties. They wanted to be sure they were in no danger. As they hopped up to the fox, he waved and said.

Fox 1: (to Hare 1 and Hare 2)

Hello, what brings you here?

Hare 1: (to Fox 1)

We just wanted to talk to you about living together in peace. We want to make sure what the rules are.

Fox 2: (to Hare 2)

What's the problem? We're not bothering you.

Hare 2: (to Fox 2)

We know, but we're always afraid of you, and we wanted to know if we could come up with a solution. Something that would put our minds at ease.

Narrator:

The foxes proposed a plan to put the hares' minds at ease.

Fox 1: (to Hare 1 and Hare 2)

We suggest that we take a pheasant from the farm.

Fox 2: (to Hare 1 and Hare 2)

You can count on us to divide the food fairly without any fights.

Narrator:

The hares were initially skeptical, but they decided to trust the foxes. A pheasant was a rare treat to eat for hares.

The foxes carried out their plan, and the hares were very grateful for their share.

Hare 1: (to Fox 1 and Fox 2)

Thank you so much for doing this for us. We can finally sleep soundly at night.

Hare 2: (to Fox 1 and Fox 2)

We never thought that we could live with foxes in peace.

Narrator:

From that day on, the hares and foxes lived in harmony and cooperation.

tHe eNd

Real-Life Examples:

1. Trying New Foods: Imagine you're at a restaurant, and your friend orders a new food you've never tried before. You might be afraid to try it because you don't know what it tastes like. But, what if it ends up being your new favorite food?

2. Meeting New People: You might be nervous about meeting a new classmate or teammate because you don't know them. But what if they end up becoming a great friend?

3. Learning a New Skill: You might be afraid to try a new sport or activity because you're not sure if you'll be good at it. But what if you discover a new talent?

Historical/Famous Examples:

1. The Story of Helen Keller: Helen Keller was born blind and deaf, but she didn't let her disabilities hold her back. She was afraid of learning at first, but with the help of her teacher, Anne Sullivan, she

discovered a new world of knowledge and communication.

2. The Story of Neil Armstrong: Neil Armstrong was the first person to walk on the moon, but he was initially afraid of the unknown dangers of space travel. However, he didn't let his fear stop him, and he went on to make history with his brave and pioneering spirit.

Discussion Questions:

1. Can you think of a time when you were afraid of something before even knowing if it was dangerous? How did it turn out?

2. Why do you think it's not good to be afraid of something before knowing the facts?

3. How can you apply this moral to your everyday life, especially when facing new or unknown situations?

Additional Tips:

1. Be Curious: Ask questions and seek out information before making judgments.

2. Take Small Steps: Start with small, manageable steps when facing a new or unknown situation.

3. Focus on the Present: Instead of worrying about what might happen, focus on what's happening right now.

Notes Page

Couplet Title:

_____

What I Learned:

_____

_____

_____

My Favorite Line:

_____

_____

_____

How I Can Apply This:

_____

_____

_____

Draw a Picture:

Additional Thoughts:

_____

_____

_____

THE CEO AND THE WORKER

Characters needed:

- Narrator
- Worker
- CEO

Narrator:

A CEO, watching his bank liquidate, was alarmed all of a sudden by the cries of another big bank purchasing it. The big bank did not offer the CEO the tax advantages and other perks he enjoyed previously. He appealed to the office workers to join in on a social media protest with him, lest they should lose their funds and services. But one worker spoke up and replied:

Worker:

Why should we worry? Do you think it is likely the new bank will treat us any differently?

CEO:

Well, no. I guess not.

Worker:

Then, as long as we have our funds, what matters to us, whom we serve?

Moral: *In a change of government, the poor change nothing beyond the name of their master.*

tHe eNd

Real-Life Examples:

1. School Leadership: Imagine your school gets a new principal. You might think that things will change for the better, but if the new principal has the same rules and policies as the old one, not much will really change for you and your friends.

2. Neighborhood Rules: Suppose your neighborhood gets a new neighborhood watch association. They might promise to make changes, but if they have the same rules and restrictions as the old association, life in the neighborhood won't change much for you and your family.

3. Company Management: Think of a company where you or your parents work. If the company gets a new president, you might hope for changes, but if the new president has the same management style and policies as the old one, not much will change for the employees.

Historical Examples:

1. Reconstruction Era: After the Civil War, the Reconstruction Era promised to bring about change and equality for African Americans. However, many of the same racist policies and laws remained in place, and the lives of many African Americans didn't change much.

2. The Freedmen's Bureau: The Freedmen's Bureau was established after the Civil War to help African Americans transition to freedom. However, the bureau was often understaffed and underfunded, and many African Americans continued to face significant challenges and injustices.

Discussion Questions:

1. Can you think of a time when a change in leadership or government didn't necessarily bring about the changes you hoped for?

2. Why do you think it's often difficult for a change in government to bring about real improvements for marginalized communities?

3. How can people work together to bring about real change and improvements in their communities?

Notes Page

Couplet Title:

_____

What I Learned:

_____

_____

_____

My Favorite Line:

_____

_____

_____

How I Can Apply This:

_____

_____

_____

Draw a Picture:

Additional Thoughts:

_____

_____

_____

MOTHER TROUT, YOUNG TROUT, AND SALMON

Character needed:

- Narrator
- Mother Trout

Narrator:

A fisherman stood angling on the bank of a river with an artificial fly.

An excellent fisherman who caught the most fish, no one could deny.

He threw his bait with so much art that a young trout was rushing towards it, when she was stopped by her mother who knew from experience when to quit.

Mother Trout:

Stop, child! Never be too quick where there is a possibility of danger.

You don't know where that treat came from, it may be from a stranger.

Take your time to consider before you risk any action that may be fatal.

One mistake and you may be seasoned and prepared on his kitchen table.

How do you know whether that is indeed a fly or the snare of an enemy?

If you look real close, you can see a man above the water, can't you see?

Let someone else do the experiment before you take that risky chance,

Swimming and trying to chase a fake fly like you are in some type of trance.

If it be a real fly, he will very probably elude the first attack,

by flying away super fast and taking away your little snack.

So, the second attempt may be made, if not with success, at least with safety.

You have to think about more important things than a treat that will be tasty.

Narrator:

As soon as she mentioned this caution, a salmon ate the fake fly and was captured.

Now, the salmon belonged to the fisherman, and to him, nothing else really mattered.

Moral: *Do not rush into a strange position.*

tHe eNd

Real-Life Examples:

1. New School Club: Imagine you're invited to join a new school club that sounds interesting, but you don't know much about it. You might be tempted to join right away, but it's better to learn more about the club and its activities before committing.

2. Online Gaming: Suppose you're playing an online game, and someone invites you to join a new server or group. You might be excited to join, but it's important to be cautious and learn more about the server or group before joining.

3. New Neighborhood: Think of a situation where your family is moving to a new neighborhood. You might be tempted to start exploring right away, but it's better to get to know the area and the people first before venturing out.

Historical/Famous Examples:

1. The Story of Harriet Tubman's Escape: Harriet Tubman, a former slave, didn't rush into her escape

from slavery. Instead, she carefully planned and prepared, using her knowledge of the Underground Railroad to make her way to freedom.

2. The Story of Langston Hughes' Career: Langston Hughes, a famous African American poet, didn't rush into his writing career. Instead, he took the time to develop his craft, learn from others, and carefully consider his words before sharing them with the world.

Discussion Questions:

1. Can you think of a time when you rushed into a situation without thinking it through? What happened?

2. Why is it important to be cautious and not rush into unfamiliar situations?

3. How can you apply this moral to your everyday life, especially when faced with new or uncertain situations?

Additional Tips:

1. Take Your Time: Don't rush into a situation without thinking it through.

2. Gather Information: Learn as much as you can about a situation before making a decision.

3. Trust Your Instincts: If something doesn't feel right, trust your instincts and be cautious.

Notes Page

Couplet Title:

_____

What I Learned:

_____

_____

_____

My Favorite Line:

_____

_____

_____

How I Can Apply This:

_____

_____

_____

Draw a Picture:

Additional Thoughts:

_____

_____

_____

THE JEALOUS TREE

Character needed:

- Narrator
- Man
- Painter
- Flower seller
- Person

Narrator:

Once, a man's foot struck against a large stone in the middle of a path.

Man:

Someone left this stone in the path of many others, but who stubs his toe? ...Me.

I'll be a good citizen, think about others, and place this huge stone by this tree.

Narrator:

A while later, a painter came to paint a painting under that tree.

Painter:

I'll paint a magnificent reddish design and then sell it for a great profit.

Paint dripped on the stone, and now it looks like real human blood is on it.

I'm walking away from this stone and paying no attention to the mess I made.

I painted a reddish design and now must leave from up under the tree's shade.

Narrator:

Sometimes later, a flower seller sat under that tree to make a flower garland. When she got up to leave, some flowers fell near the stone.

Flower seller:

I'll weave these flowers together in a cornrow braid with a gold ribbon going through it.

I like to make my holiday wreaths pretty, with bright colors that combine to make a unit.

Narrator:

All the town's people started worshiping the stone, and thought it was an idol from God. The tree grew jealous. He thought, "People come to offer prayers to the stone. Before this, they used to come to sit in my shade." So, the tree picked up the stone and flung it far away. When the people came to offer prayers, they found the stone missing. They said:

Person:

If God left this place, then this place must be unholy, and so is this tree.

If we cut the tree down now, I doubt anyone from town would disagree.

Narrator:

So the tree finally understood the moral of this short story, as they cut it down. With its dying breath, the tree thought, "Ah! Now I am getting punished for being jealous."

tHe eNd

Real-Life Examples:

1. School Sports: Imagine you're on a school sports team, and one of your teammates is getting more attention from the coach. You might feel jealous and start to act out, but that could get you in trouble.

2. *Friendship*: Suppose your best friend starts hanging out with someone new, and you feel left out. You might get jealous and try to sabotage their new friendship, but that could damage your relationship with your friend.

3. Classroom: Think of a situation where a classmate gets praised by the teacher for their work, and you feel jealous. You might start to act out or try to one-up them, but that could get you in trouble.

Historical/Famous Examples:

1. The Story of Madam C.J. Walker and Annie Malone: Madam C.J. Walker and Annie Malone were two African American entrepreneurs who

developed successful hair care businesses in the early 20th century. However, their rivalry and jealousy towards each other led to a public feud.

2. The Story of Thurgood Marshall and the NAACP: Thurgood Marshall was a prominent African American lawyer who argued several landmark civil rights cases before the Supreme Court. However, he faced jealousy and criticism from some of his colleagues within the NAACP, who questioned his methods and motives.

Discussion Questions:

1. Can you think of a time when you felt jealous? How did you handle it?

2. Why do you think jealousy can be a problem?

3. How can you work on managing your jealousy in a healthy way?

Additional Tips:

1. Recognize Your Feelings: When you start to feel jealous, take a step back and acknowledge your emotions.

2. Talk to Someone: Share your feelings with a trusted friend, family member, or teacher.

3. Focus on Your Own Strengths: Instead of comparing yourself to others, focus on your own strengths and accomplishments.

Notes Page

Couplet Title:

_____

What I Learned:

_____

_____

_____

My Favorite Line:

_____

_____

_____

How I Can Apply This:

_____

_____

_____

Draw a Picture:

Additional Thoughts:

_____

_____

_____

THE FOX AND THE GRAPES

Characters needed:

- Narrator
- Fox

Narrator:

A Fox, one day, looked up high and spied a beautiful bunch of juicy, ripe grapes.

He was hungry and wanted desperately to collect them without any mistakes.

They hung from a vine around the branches of a tree.

Fox

All those purple grapes must surely be waiting for me.

Narrator:

The plump, luscious grapes seemed ready to burst with juice.

Fox remembered that taste, but just remembering was no use.

Fox's mouth watered as he gazed longingly at them.

Fox:

I love purple grapes, and I'll suck them right off the stem.

Narrator:

The grapes hung from a branch high up on a branch of an old tree.

Fox stared at the juicy, ripe grapes, but staring did not get them free.

Then Fox jumped straight up, really high for the ripe fruit.

The animals took pictures; a jumping fox looked real cute.

On his first jump, he missed the grapes by a long way.

He thought, by now, he would be eating grapes today.

So he walked off a half mile and took a running leap.

He thought a paw full of grapes he'd be able to keep.

But he realized that he fell short, and he failed once more.

His stomach began to cramp and ache, right at the core.

Again and again he tried for grapes, but no luck, all in vain.

Now, the cramping and ache in his stomach turned into pain.

Fox looked at the grapes in anger and disgust.

His ability to jump high, he could no longer trust.

Fox

What a fool I am, jumping for grapes, with all my power.

Those grapes look real good, but they probably taste sour.

Narrator:

He stated them being sour, sarcastically.

But off he walked very, very scornfully.

Moral: *There are many who pretend to despise and belittle that which is beyond their reach.*

tHe eNd

Real-Life Examples:

1. Schoolyard Teasing: Imagine someone in your school is teasing you about something you have or something you're good at. They might be saying mean things because they're jealous or feel left out.

2. Social Media: Suppose someone is posting mean comments about someone else's accomplishments or possessions on social media. They might be trying to make themselves feel better by belittling someone else.

3. Classroom Envy: Think of a situation where a classmate is envious of your grades or academic achievements. They might start to belittle your accomplishments or make fun of you.

Historical/Famous Examples:

1. The Story of Crispus Attucks: Crispus Attucks was an African American man who was a hero of the American Revolution. However, some people at

the time tried to belittle his contributions and bravery because of his skin color.

2. The Story of Bessie Coleman: Bessie Coleman was a pioneering African American pilot who faced racism and sexism in her career. Some people tried to belittle her accomplishments and question her abilities because of her gender and skin color.

Discussion Questions:

1. Can you think of a time when someone tried to belittle or mock something you were proud of? How did you feel?

2. Why do you think some people try to belittle or mock things they don't understand or can't have?

3. How can you respond when someone tries to belittle or mock you or something you're proud of?

Additional Tips:

1. Stay Confident: Don't let someone else's negativity bring you down. Stay confident and proud of your accomplishments.

2. Ignore the Haters: Sometimes, it's best to just ignore people who are trying to belittle or mock you.

3. Surround Yourself with Positive People: Spend time with people who support and encourage you, rather than those who try to bring you down.

Notes Page

Couplet Title:

_____

What I Learned:

_____

_____

_____

My Favorite Line:

_____

_____

_____

How I Can Apply This:

_____

_____

_____

Draw a Picture:

Additional Thoughts:

_____

_____

_____

A LION IN LOVE

Characters needed:

- Narrator

- Lion

- Beautiful Maiden

- Fox

Narrator:

Twenty score and seven years ago, a lion fell in love with a beautiful maiden. Not only was she beautiful, but she was very athletic and played a harmonica just for fun. One day this beautiful maiden walked into the jungle to find some fresh berries for a pie and sassafras root for some tea.

As she walked deeper into the jungle and played on the harmonica, a ferocious lion saw her and began to stalk her.

As the lion crept behind her, ready to pounce on her and eat her up, the lion noticed how beautiful she looked. Her athletic body, wonderful playing of music, and her long braids made the maiden even more desirable. The lion had never heard music like that and fell immediately and completely in love.

Now, the lion wanted to marry the beautiful maiden instead of eating her. So he brushed the fur out of his face, stood up straight on his hind legs, and boldly went to speak to the beautiful maiden.

Lion:

Excuse me, pretty lady, do you have a second or two?

I heard your beautiful playing and wanted to meet you.

You are really beautiful, and I like your rendition of that song.

I wanted to ask a few questions, and I will not keep you long.

I would like us to get to know each other because I can listen to you forever.

This is my question to you: do you think you and I have a chance to get together?

Beautiful Maiden:

…Get together? What on Earth are you talking about? Playing cards, having lunch, Bible study, what?

Lion:

Well, yes, if that is what you want to do.

I just want to spend quality time with you.

I would like for you to first, be my girlfriend

Take my paw and my love to you I'll extend.

After a while, marry me so we can have many offspring.

I would be your king of beasts and would give you anything.

We can travel this world together and not have to be so careful.

Me plus you, means our little ones will be beautiful and powerful!

Beautiful Maiden:

LOL. Silly boy, you are a lion. An animal. I am human. Humans cannot marry animals! You are too funny. LOL

Narrator:

The beautiful maiden walked off laughing, and the lion fell into a deep depression and became completely hopeless. He walked away crying and feeling sorry for himself. It was a sad scene to see.

A fox came along, saw the sad, crying lion, and asked:

Fox:

What is going on with you today, bro lion? You look so sad and down.

I've never seen a lion cry, never seen one sad, nor even with a frown.

Lion:

I asked that beautiful maiden to be my girlfriend, with the hopes that she would want to marry me.

I didn't mean to diminish your impression of me. But she is so beautiful, wouldn't you agree?

Fox:

LOL.

You are an old fool in love. That woman doesn't want to have a family with a lion.

She is a human and out of your league, so I'm not sure why you are even trying.

One day you will wonder which left turn in the past you took.

But if you ask me, just think how ugly your children would look.

Lion:

I guess you are right, but she is so young and beautiful. I thought I loved her!

My mind was blown, and you woke me up, so I just want to say thank you, sir.

Fox:

Forget about your love for that woman, and remember your identity as the king of beasts!

You rule all the animals and the land we see, from the North, South, West, and East.

Here you are, crying, trying to fall in love and snuggle.

But you have responsibilities as King of this Jungle!

Lion:

Yeah, I see my mistake, and I see you are right.

I was lost in deep love, but now I see the light.

Narrator:

The lion heeded the fox's advice and returned to his life as a strong and powerful beast, accepting his animal identity.

Moral: Love can sometimes make us lose sight of who we are, but it is important to stay true to ourselves and not forget our own worth and purpose.

tHe eNd

Real-Life Examples:

1. Romantic Relationships: Imagine you're in a relationship, and you start to change who you are to please your partner. You might start to dress differently, like different music, or hang out with different friends. But in doing so, you might lose sight of who you are and what makes you happy.

2. Friendships: Suppose you have a friend who is really popular, and you start to change your behavior to fit in with their crowd. You might start to do things you don't really want to do or pretend to like things you don't really like. But in doing so, you might lose sight of what's important to you.

3. Family Relationships: Think of a situation where a family member is trying to control your life or change who you are. They might be pushing you to pursue a certain career or hobby or trying to dictate what you wear or how you look. But it's essential to remember that you have your own worth and

purpose, and you shouldn't let someone else define that for you.

Historical/Famous Examples:

1. The Story of Rosa Parks: Rosa Parks was a civil rights activist who refused to give up her seat on a bus to a white person. She stayed true to herself and her values, even in the face of adversity.

2. The Story of Maya Angelou: Maya Angelou was a renowned poet and author who overcame many challenges in her life, including racism and personal struggles. She stayed true to herself and her art and became a powerful voice for marginalized communities.

Discussion Questions:

1. Can you think of a time when you felt pressure to change who you are to fit in with someone else? How did you handle it?

2. Why is it essential to stay true to ourselves and not forget our own worth and purpose?

3. How can you prioritize your own needs and desires in relationships with others?

Additional Tips:

1. Self-Reflection: Take time to reflect on your values, goals, and aspirations. What makes you happy? What's important to you?

2. Boundary Setting: Learn to set healthy boundaries with others. It's okay to say no or set limits when necessary.

3. Surround Yourself with Positive Influences: Spend time with people who support and encourage you to be your authentic self.

These examples and discussion questions can help 6th graders understand the moral and how it applies to real-life situations, both historically and today.

Notes Page

Couplet Title:

_____

What I Learned:

_____

_____

_____

My Favorite Line:

_____

_____

_____

How I Can Apply This:

_____

_____

_____

Draw a Picture:

Additional Thoughts:

_____

_____

_____

Bonus Preview:

DOG AND A JUICY BONE

Characters needed:
- Narrator
- Dog
- Frog

Narrator:

There once was a greedy dog that found a bone with some meat still on it, wet.

She grabbed the bone, to take back home to see how much meat she could get.

Crossing a bridge, she glanced into a pond and was shocked by her reflection.

That was enough to change her mind and send her thinking in a new direction.

No longer did she want to get on home and chew on her new found meaty prize.

She now wanted to threaten and take a bone, from a dog about her same size.

She barked super loud to jack the tasty treat, from the mouth of the other dog.

Her juicy bone fell in the pond, and then she heard laughter, from a nearby frog.

Frog:

"You dogs are so greedy, you didn't realize that was your reflection, in the water."

"I've seen this so many times, for every bone down there, I wish I had a quarter. "

Dog:

"Don't rub it in. I lost my bone, you talking quarters, I don't even have one red penny.

"I should have been happy with the juicy bone I had, because now I don't have any."

tHe eNd

About Author: Ricki Connor

- Creative Director/Writer, metaScreenPlays LLC

- Son, Brother, Husband, Father, Grandfather

- MAT - Educational Technology, MBA

- 30+ years IT

- 6 years USMC Reserves

metaScreenPlays - Learn, Create, Inspire

Learn More

metaScreenPlays.com:

- Subsequent volumes

- Blogs

- Articles

Ideas for fundraisers using this book

Creating fundraisers using children's books of poems written as stage-ready scripts can be a fun and engaging way for teachers, parents, and daycare givers to raise money. Here are some steps to consider:

1. Select the Poems

- Choose a collection of poems from our children's poems/stories and allow children to explore the different roles. Ensure a Director is chosen to help young actors perform and understand the clear themes or messages.

2. Create a Performance Plan

- Format: Decide on the format of the performance. Will it be a play, a talent show, a poetry reading, or a combination?
- Roles: Assign roles to children based on their interests and abilities, ensuring everyone has a chance to participate.

3. Rehearsals

- Plan regular rehearsals to help children become comfortable with their parts. This also builds teamwork and confidence.

4. Set a Performance Date and Location

- Choose a date that works for everyone involved. Consider hosting the event at a school, community center, or even outdoors if weather permits.

5. Promote the Event

- Create flyers, posters, and social media posts to advertise the event. Highlight the unique aspect of the performance being based on children's poetry.

6. Ticket Sales

- Charge for tickets to the performance. Consider offering family packages or discounts for early purchases.
- You can also sell refreshments or merchandise related to the performance (like copies of our book).

7. Engage the Community

- Reach out to local businesses for sponsorships or donations. They could contribute by covering costs or providing prizes for a raffle.

8. Incorporate Interactive Elements

- Include activities for children during the event, such as poetry workshops, art stations, or themed games, to enhance the experience.

9. Document the Performance

- Consider recording the performance or taking photos to create a keepsake for participants. This can also be used for future promotions.

10. Follow Up

- Thank everyone who participated and supported the event. Share the results of the fundraiser and how the funds will be used.

Additional Ideas

- Online Performances: If in-person gatherings are challenging, consider hosting a virtual performance to reach a wider audience.
- Themed Events: Create a theme around the poems (e.g., nature, friendship) to make the event more engaging.

By combining creativity with community involvement, these fundraisers can be both successful and enriching for everyone involved! Feel free to email

us questions: metaScreenPlays@gmail.com

Now your turn

Enhance your creativity and develop your unique voice in poetry!

Use these tools and techniques to enhance your creative writing:

Poetry Writing Checklist

Tools

1. Notebook or Journal

   * Keep a dedicated space for ideas, drafts, and finished poems.

2. Pencil/Pen

   * Use different colors for brainstorming and drafting ideas to make the writing process fun.

3. Dictionary/Thesaurus

   * Explore word meanings and find synonyms to expand vocabulary.

4. Rhyme Dictionary

   * Use an online or physical rhyme dictionary to find perfect rhymes for words.

5. Online Resources

   * Access websites and apps dedicated to poetry prompts and examples.

6. Recording Device

   * Use a smartphone or audio recorder to capture spontaneous ideas or readings of poems.

7. Art Supplies

   * Incorporate drawings or collages that inspire your writing.

 Techniques

1. Imagery

   * Use descriptive language to create vivid images in the reader's mind.

2. Metaphors and Similes

   * Compare two unlike things to add depth and understanding (e.g., "Life is a journey"). Look up the definition of these words.

3. Alliteration

* Use repeated consonant sounds at the beginning of words for rhythm (e.g., "whispering winds").

4. Personification

* Give human qualities to nonhuman things to create connection (e.g., "The sun smiled down").

5. Sound Devices

* Experiment with assonance, consonance, and onomatopoeia to enhance the musicality of the poem. Look up the definition of these words.

6. Line Breaks

* Use line breaks strategically to create pauses and emphasize certain words or ideas.

7. Form and Structure

  * Explore different poetic forms (haiku, limerick, free

verse) to find your unique style.

8. Theme Exploration

  * Choose a theme to focus on, such as nature, love, or

friendship, to give direction to your writing.

9. Sensory Details

  * Incorporate sights, sounds, smells, tastes, and textures

to engage readers' senses.

10. Revision Techniques

  * Read poems aloud to hear how they sound, and

revise based on flow and clarity.

11. Writing Prompts

   * Use creative prompts to spark ideas (e.g., "Write a poem about your favorite season").

12. Collaboration

   * Share poems with friends or family for feedback and inspiration.

13. Reading Aloud

   * Read poems by other poets to understand different styles and techniques.

14. Mind Mapping

   * Create visual maps of ideas related to a topic to brainstorm and organize thoughts.

15. Journaling

* Write daily reflections to practice expression and develop ideas for poems.

Join the Journey

Stay tuned for future volumes, as we continue to unlock the wisdom of Aesop's Fables. Together, let's inspire creative youth to become empathetic, thoughtful, and compassionate individuals.

metaScreenPlays - Learn, Create, Inspire

metaScreenPlays.com

metaScreenPlays@gmail.com